# THE HAINDL TAROT DECK

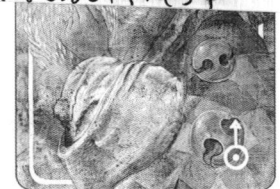

Created by HERMANN HAINDL

Booklet based on
*The Haindl Tarot* vols. 1 & 2,
by RACHEL POLLACK

U.S. GAMES SYSTEMS, INC.
Publishers
Stamford, CT 06902 USA

Copyright © 1990 by
U.S. GAMES SYSTEMS, INC.

All rights reserved. The illustrations, cover design and contents are protected by copyright. No part of this booklet may be reproduced in any form without permission in writing from the publisher, except by a reviewer who wishes to quote brief passages in connection with a review written for inclusion in a magazine or newspaper.

10 9 8

Made in Italy

U.S. GAMES SYSTEMS, INC.
179 Ludlow Street
Stamford, CT 06902 USA

# THE HAINDL TAROT DECK

## INTRODUCTION

The complete seventy-eight-card tarot pack is divided into two sections: twenty-two Major Arcana and fifty-six Minor Arcana cards. The Major Arcana are twenty-two trump cards, usually numbered 0 through 21 and displaying names such as "The Empress" or "The Fool." The Minor Arcana contain four suits of fourteen cards each, ace through ten and four "court" cards: traditionally, king, queen, knight or prince, and page or princess. The court cards of the Haindl Tarot are mother (queen), father (king), daughter (princess) and son (prince). The traditional tarot suits are swords, wands or staves, cups and coins. The Haindl Tarot replaces the suit of coins with the suit of stones.

The Haindl Tarot deck is rich with symbolism, emotion and mythology. A single gesture, or an object, or a color pattern will appear simple, but will actually convey a whole range of ideas. Contemplating a card, the reader can learn much, even without the aid of text. However, as a person can appreciate nature without understanding its inner workings, a friendly guide can deepen and expand that appreciation by pointing out details that could be missed and by illuminating hidden aspects. So, Rachel Pollack's book, *The Haindl Tarot*, is a friend, a guide for the Haindl Tarot. This booklet is extracted from the Pollack book, providing a starting point for those who wish to explore the beauty and depth of the Haindl Tarot.

The divinatory interpretations of the cards may at times seem contradictory. This is because each meaning contains the suggestion to look within to realize the positive potential expressed in the card, or to become aware of the negative potential and transform it to the positive.

## THE MAJOR ARCANA

On each Major Arcana card is a Hebrew letter, a rune and an astrological sign. The inner borders of the cards represent the four elements, with white for air, blue for water, red for fire and yellow for earth. The descriptions give the Hebrew letter and its meaning, the rune and its meaning, and the astrological sign.

**0 THE FOOL** Aleph, ox; Wynn, W, joy; Uranus. The Fool is a medieval court jester, required to entertain, but also to speak truths no one else would care to express. The wounded swan represents the fall from grace, the parting of humanity from the Garden of Eden. At the bottom is Earth. **Divinatory meanings:** Act impulsively. Follow your feelings. Surprise. Wonder. Excitement. Take opportunities that arise. **Reversed:** Difficulty believing in your instincts. Fear of stepping into the unknown. Do not be reckless.

**I THE MAGICIAN** Beth, house; Peoh, P, cattle or property; Mercury. The symbols in the foreground represent the four suits of the Minor Arcana: wands, swords, cups and stones. They are also ritual objects for the Holy Grail. The Magician wears a tiara, symbol of the crowning power of the intellect. Crystals radiating from the Magician's left eye indicate the ability to perceive the pure forms of existence, an ability that could be clouded by unintegrated darker emotions, represented by the figure rising from the tiara. **Divinatory meanings:** Power. Strength. Being in control of one's life. Transforming old situations, bringing in new ones. A burst of energy. Creativity. Focused will. **Reversed:** Natural expression of energy blocked. Inner resistance. Arrogance. Misuse of personal power.

**II THE HIGH PRIESTESS** Gimel, camel; Ur, U, bison or rain; Moon. The High Priestess is the Goddess, manifested as the moon, the seas, the night and the Earth. Light fills the card, radiating from her palms, pouring down from a globe over her head. Her dress seems to pour down like rain on the camel and the dark land. She is the divine life principle. **Divinatory meanings:** A time for quiet, for looking inward. Seek peace. Use intuition and feeling. Peace and joy. Possibly, a lover who needs solitude or is avoiding commitment. **Reversed:** A time for action, for involvements with others. Commitment in romance.

**III THE EMPRESS** Daleth, door; Thorn, T, thunder or door; Earth. Below the eye at the top of the card is a woman and behind her, a doorway symbolizing culture.

The open door is scaled, like a fish, and the arch suggests a church, religion. The woman stands on a crescent that floats in the water. She holds a scepter topped with a pine cone and a snake that wraps around her arm. The snake represents transformation and enlightenment. A band of light is around her head. A golden bird flies toward her ear, as if to bring the word of heaven. **Divinatory meanings:** Passion. Love of nature. Motherhood. Joyous activity. **Reversed:** Passion blocked. Difficulty expressing oneself. Problems with one's mother.

**IV THE EMPEROR** Heh, window; Ansuz, A, stag, or Ansur, mouth; Aries. The tree behind the Emperor is Yggdrasil, the world tree of Scandinavian myth, with its roots deep in the mysterious origins of life and its branches reaching up to the stars and beyond. The Emperor holds the rod he received from the Empress. The gold ball in his other hand symbolizes the material world. The diamond overhead contains the colors of humanity. **Divinatory meanings:** Influence of society, law. Resurgence of energy. Sexual potency. Arrogance. Insensitivity. Energy and desire. **Reversed:** Blocked possibility. Development of sensitivity.

**V THE HIEROPHANT** Vav, nail; Radh, R, wheel; Taurus. A grandfather fills most of the picture. To his right appears the father. At the bottom is the back of a boy's head. The boy wears a skullcap. The three generations of men represent the positive value of patriarchal religion and Judaism, the "father" of both Christianity and Islam. The book and the key before it symbolize the Torah, the five books of Moses and the "key" to Jewish culture. The book also symbolizes culture and knowledge. **Divinatory meanings:** Tradition, community and teachings. Conformity. Marriage, or any solemn commitment. **Reversed:** Social pressure. Doctrines and ideas that have lost meaning. Originality. Gullibility.

**VI THE LOVERS** Zain, sword; Ken, K, torch; Gemini. The Lovers cross arms behind a cup. In the sky is a spear, a unicorn and a rose within a Star of David. The trees on either side refer to the Garden of Eden, with the Tree of Life and the Tree of Knowledge. The woman's hair is like pitted rock, a sign of the ancientness of human sexual traditions. The ground shows the earthiness of love; the unicorn and the rose reflect its mystical qualities. **Divinatory meanings:** The importance of love. Depending on the place in the spread, the state of a specific relationship. **Reversed:** A relationship ending. Trouble in a relationship. Lack of love. Insecurity, loneliness. Loss of balance.

**VII THE CHARIOT** Cheth, fence; Hagall, H, hailstone; Cancer. A boat with wheels rushes through a rough sea. The boat is red, the color of energy. A red glow surrounds the figure in the boat. Above is a mythical beast, part boar, part wolf. It signifies our deepest fears, unnameable and wild. **Divinatory meanings:** Willpower in dealing with problems. Will to continue. Deep fear driving a person. Triumph over fear. **Reversed:** Lack of will. Passivity or weakness. It may be best to let things run their course.

**VIII STRENGTH** Teth, snake; Sigil, S, sun; Leo. The person of Strength is open, without shame. Her strength comes from her unity with Earth and her own divine energy. She is a shaman performing a ritual under the moon, in the woods by a pool of water. The pool is the unconscious, the hidden mysteries. By holding up the snake, the shaman connects the above and the below, the sky and the Earth. The snake is green, the color of new life, and its underside is red, the color of energy. **Divinatory meanings:** Inner strength. Love and gentleness. Confidence. Ability to give love. **Reversed:** Feeling blocked from one's power. Weak. Overwhelmed. Meditation or some form of relaxation may help restore strength.

**IX THE HERMIT** Yod, hand; Is, I, ice; Virgo. A man stands on a mountaintop, surrounded by birds symbolizing the spirit. The gnomes, whose faces appear in the rocks, symbolize the elemental spirit forces alive in nature. The lantern is human knowledge and teachings passed from generation to generation. An eye inside a triangle forms a traditional image of God. **Divinatory meanings:** Withdrawal from outside interests. Self-reliance. Self-creation. Developing one's personality. Gaining wisdom. Powerful dreams. **Reversed:** Involvement with others. Fear of loneliness. Disturbing dreams. A desire not to grow up.

**X THE WHEEL OF FORTUNE** Kaph, palm; Jara or Ger, J, year; Jupiter. The Wheel is set against a field of stars symbolizing the cosmos. Below, looking upward, is the Mother, the Earth. At the upper left is the Sky Father, Zeus. At the upper right is an androgynous child. The child, with its wizened face, represents humanity and our ancestors. Inside the Wheel, the mushrooms symbolize luck, the snake, rebirth, the eye, time, the dinosaur, all things lost in the turning of time. **Divinatory meanings:** Change of circumstances. Taking hold of one's life. Grabbing hold of fate. Time to take what life has given you. **Reversed:** Difficulty adjusting to changes. Resistance to change.

**XI JUSTICE** Lamed, ox goad; Nyd, N, necessity; Libra. Two separate images of balance are made by the scales in the foreground and the peacock feathers. The scales hang from an invisible holder, unchanging, the cosmic balls suspended above the pans. This signifies that Justice always exists in the universe as a perfect principle. The feathers exist in a much more precarious balance; a breath of wind would disrupt them. In the world of ordinary experience, Justice often seems remote. The feathers appear rooted in a tree trunk, suggesting that spirit does not exist apart from nature. Their "eyes" signify seeing our own emotions. **Divinatory meanings:** Examine your life, weigh things in the balance. A relationship is going badly. Analysis. Take a balanced view. **Reversed:** Do not act out of habit. Imbalance. You may be acting unfairly. Trying to avoid an honest evaluation.

**XII THE HANGED MAN** Mem, seas; Tyr or Tewaz, T, a war god or god of law; Neptune. The Hanged Man is Odin of Scandinavian myth. The rainbow implies water; its colors also correspond to the Hanged Man's body to the chakras, yogic points of energy in the human physique. The Hanged Man's hair seems to merge into the ground like the roots of a tree. On one side shines a crescent moon, symbol of the High Priestess, goddess of mystery. On the other appear Odin's twin ravens, Hugin and Munin, thought and memory. Ravens signify death and thus bring information from the "other world." **Divinatory meanings:** Attachment. Deep spiritual awareness. Independence. **Reversed:** Being overly influenced by outside ideas. Pressure to conform. Demands. Sacrificing something to get past hangups. Lack of purpose.

**XIII DEATH** Nun, fish; Ba or Beorc, B, birch goddess or boat; Scorpio. The image of the boat belongs to birth as well as to death; the baby's cradle originally symbolized a boat. The trees and grass signify plants, the bones, minerals, the birds, the animal world, and the ferryman, the human world. The peacock's eye in the center signifies looking at the truth in regard to death. The bird also symbolizes the soul and the divine potential of a person. **Divinatory meanings:** The Death card rarely refers to physical death. Rather, it has to do with one's feelings about death. Psychologically, letting go. New opportunities. **Reversed:** Resisting change. Stagnation. Inertia. Pain of giving something up.

**XIV ALCHEMY** Samekh, tent peg; Laguz, L, water; Sagittarius. The diagonal divides the card between blue and red, water and fire. The Grail appears twice, red in the blue half, and blue in the red half, providing an interchange of energy. The two cups come from the traditional image of the card as Temperance. On the right a circle contains the sun and the moon. The red background is pitted rock, a symbol of age. The blue side is ageless light, a quality of spirit. A devil face inhabits the cloud, signifying sexual life energy. On the other side is her reflection, an angel. Below the angel and the devil is a clown and a skull, life and death. **Divinatory meanings:** Measurement and combination. Do not allow setbacks to turn enthusiasm into its mirror image of dejection. Take control. Moderation. **Reversed:** Going to extremes. Excessive behavior. Conserve energy. A person out of control.

**XV THE DEVIL** Ayin, eye; Eolh, elk or man; Capricorn. The picture is organized around a diagonal line, broken by a crystal, which transforms the aggressive instinct of the Devil. The snake is an image of rebirth and the visionary experience, and also of evil. The Devil has three horns and three eyes, and wears a stone diadem.

8

**Divinatory meanings:** Something exciting, possibly dangerous or forbidden. Temptation. Physical gratification. Exploring darker feelings. Wild action opens up new areas in life. **Reversed:** Resisting temptation. Not a time for sensuality. Fear of one's own decisions.

**XVI THE TOWER** Peh, mouth; Yr or Irr, to err; Mars. The Tower symbolizes an arrogant technology that constantly desires more and bigger monuments to its conquest of nature. Inside of it is darkness and fire. It is a modern image of the Tower of Babel. The sunrise and blue sky suggest hope. **Divinatory meanings:** Long-standing activity or approach that may bring about disaster if continued. Pressure building up. Long-buried emotions let loose. News. A flash of understanding. **Reversed:** Similar to upright meanings, but less severe. A shaking up. Minor disturbance.

**XVII THE STAR** Tzaddi, fish hook; Eh, E, horse; Aquarius. A woman is at the bottom of a bare rocky hill where a stream of water splashes into a pool. She is washing her hair, an act of unity with the Earth. Her hair blends into the water. Her dress suggests age. She is Gaia, the Mother of Life. No flowers or trees grow, there are only water and rock, Earth's oldest forms. Above her is a cluster of stars, seven small ones and one large double star. **Divinatory meanings:** Renewal. Reality and feeling. Cleansing. Humility. Hope. **Reversed:** Fears for the future. Isolation. Tension or anxiety. Hope.

**XVIII THE MOON** Kaph, back of head; Othal, O, prosperity; Pisces. The landscape represents peace, while the lobster represents fear. The unicorn, which replaces the traditional dog and wolf, is the imagination. The entire image is dreamy and surrealistic, a land of myths, illusions and wonders, the path of the imagination which can lead to perfect knowledge. **Divinatory meanings:** Imagination. Fantasies, daydreams, strong dreams. The sources of creativity. **Reversed:** The time to return to "solar," rational activities. Conscious mind blocking the unconscious.

**XIX THE SUN** Resh, head; Gebo, G, gift; Sun. The Sun is a labyrinth of spirals, the trees line up with an order never found in nature, and the rose appears as dreamlike. We have not returned to the ordinary world, but have moved to another level of myth. The Sun shows an idea of nature, not nature itself. **Divinatory meanings:** Joy and simplicity. Life is wonderful. Energy. Activity, excitement, optimism. Rational approach. Confidence. Sexual desire. **Reversed:** Sun is clouded over. Day-to-day problems, though happiness remains. Loss of confidence. Frustration.

**XX AEON** Shin, tooth; Peorth, P, secret; Pluto. While at the bottom is a clear landscape, the sky is obscured with dark clouds—an unknown and ominous future. The rivers run through canyons of great age. The land is dark but green. On the left is a blasted tree, on the right, shadows. Beyond the flat land are hills and white mountains, symbols of purity and abstract truth. A dark volcano, destruction, looms behind the mountains. The shape of the head is birdlike but the eye is human. It is the Goddess, a woman as the Earth, a bird as the sky, ancient and suffering. The baby in the center represents hope of renewal. **Divinatory meanings:** Renewal. Optimism, in spite of a painful period of change. Change. Spontaneity. All things are possible. Old world seen through new eyes. **Reversed:** Rebirth. Resisting change. A new life, possibly not acknowledged.

**XXI THE UNIVERSE** Tav, signature; Gebo, G, gift; Saturn. The Earth, whose bottom half shows, is circled by a dragon. Both are green, the color of new life. The fire is red, color of energy and blood, and white, color of pure thought. The serpent's breath burns away illusion. **Divinatory meanings:** Success. Becoming happier, more fulfilled. Recovery from illness. An exciting future. Satisfaction. Justified pride. Life opening up. **Reversed:** Stagnation. Lack of willpower and confidence. Self-defined limitations. Resistance or opposition.

## THE MINOR ARCANA: The Numbered Cards

The suits of the Minor Arcana are situated east (wands) for India, north (cups) for the Celtic countries, south (swords) for Egypt and west (stones) for North America. An I Ching symbol, called a hexagram, appears on the numbered cards two through ten. The descriptions give the number and title of each hexagram, as assigned by Wilhelm. The titles on the cards them-

## THE SUIT OF WANDS

**ACE OF WANDS** The "lingam" and the "yoni," the phallic stone and the pool of water, the male and female aspects of God, mix on the ace of wands. **Divinatory meanings:** Gift of fire. Energy, optimism, confidence. Desire. Beginnings. **Reversed:** Lack of focus. Scattered or confused efforts. Pessimism.

**TWO OF WANDS** 26 The Taming Power of the Great. The setting of a ruined church indicates the power of the soul. A staircase is a spiritual ascent. Two crossed spears form a symbol of power and pacification. **Divinatory meanings:** Power. Strong will. The power of spiritual truth. **Reversed:** Voluntarily giving up a position of power. Seeking adventures. Misuse of power.

**THREE OF WANDS** 50 The Cauldron. The ruined cathedral's window opens to the sky. The remains suggest humanity's ancient need to give structure to religious feeling. **Divinatory meanings:** Acting in harmony with nature. Purpose. Good fortune. **Reversed:** Being out of harmony with the situation. Difficulty in finding the point of life or in discovering worthy goals.

**FOUR OF WANDS** 63 After Completion. A hand offers a bubble in the middle of which is an eye. The bubble indicates new possibilities. The spears pointing up and down are perfectly balanced energies. **Divinatory meanings:** New life. Take action at the right moment. Excitement and growth. **Reversed:** Errors. Impatient for new start. Wait for genuine opportunity.

**FIVE OF WANDS** 49 Revolution. The top of the phallic stone column resembles a brain, suggesting the human body. The dark, chaotic column suggests bloody history. The arrangement of the spears is hierarchical. **Divinatory meanings:** Strife and battle, without hatred or bitterness. Avoidance. **Reversed:** Personal and aggressive conflicts. Bitterness toward others.

**SIX OF WANDS** 2 The Receptive. The six spears are at the same height, suggesting cooperation. Vines of ivy signify victory; as evergreens they triumph over the death of winter. **Divinatory meanings:** Triumph. Confidence and firm action will lead to triumph. Inspiration. **Reversed:** Loss of belief. Negative attitude can lead to failure.

**SEVEN OF WANDS** 40 Liberation. The scene is peaceful, though the sky is cloudy. The spears rise out of holes in the rock, active humanity striving upward. The ball above is the nonmaterial world of the mystic. **Divinatory meanings:** Courage and daring—possibly the courage to retreat. Using one's power for transformation. **Reversed:** Loss of nerve. Hesitation. Seek an alternative, possibly reconciliation.

**EIGHT OF WANDS** 35 Progress. The spears move upward, for spiritual development. Red, as of fire or blood, gives way to blue sky. The impulse for movement comes from life energy but carries us to a purer level. The spears move jointly, energy focused on a single goal. **Divinatory meanings:** Definite movement. Progress. A worthy goal. Finding direction in life. Development of a new love affair. **Reversed:** Scattered energy. Contradictory activities. Fear of taking action. Shyness, or jealousy.

**NINE OF WANDS** 7 The Army. The thrusting spears are an image of bursting energy. The tree reflects the energy, and also is the power of nature. **Divinatory meanings:** Great energy. Arrogance, especially toward those who feel weak. Life's resiliency. **Reversed:** Weakness. Passivity. Arrogance or misuse of power.

**TEN OF WANDS** 54 The Marrying Maiden. The background shows a bat, a flying mouse, swooping down on frightened cats, a reversal of power. Hope is shown by the feathers on the bat's wings, indicating that the bat may transform into a bird, symbol of spirituality. Oppression is giving way to wisdom. **Divinatory meanings:** Oppression. Depression. Transformation from cruelty to liberation. Possible fall. **Reversed:** Emerging from a bad situation. Wisdom gained from adversity.

## THE SUIT OF CUPS

**ACE OF CUPS** A simple cup is formed of spiraling gold, symbolizing spiritual evolution. A single drop, tinged with red, falls into the cup. It is life. **Divinatory meanings:** Happiness. Love, joy, optimism. Love flowing openly between two people. **Reversed:** Happiness is blocked. Trouble communicating. Value of life questioned.

**TWO OF CUPS** 1 The Creative. The peacock symbolizes rebirth and balance. It is a fantasy bird, emphasizing the importance of fantasy in love. Two cups show two people joining together in love. **Divinatory meanings:** Relationship. Possibly, the need to make a commitment. **Reversed:** Quarreling or jealousy. Uncertain future. Lack of commitment.

**THREE OF CUPS** 28 Preponderance of the Great. Three cups are in an upward pointing triangle symbolic of fire. The cave indicates that the card deals with inner experience. Rocks at the bottom hint of danger; however, the cups overflow with joy. **Divinatory meanings:** Great feeling. Extreme joy that can turn to tears. **Reversed:** Feelings dammed up. Instability.

**FOUR OF CUPS** 3 Difficulties at the Beginning. An autumn scene is sad, but sweet. It describes the possibilities of growth from a situation that appears dark and heavy. **Divinatory meanings:** Find a moment of peace and balance. Action is possible and will lead to growth. **Reversed:** Loss of balance. Suppressed emotions.

**FIVE OF CUPS** 9 The Taming Power of the Small. Brown, bare rock suggests unfulfilled hopes. The water is a thin stream, disappointment. A single cup catches the water, and so the experience has not been wasted. **Divinatory meanings:** Be patient. Confusion and disappointment are exaggerated. **Reversed:** Coming out of disappointment. A realistic view of the past.

**SIX OF CUPS** 58 The Joyous Lake. The column is part of a temple. The bubble is tinted red, for life energy. A five-pointed star indicates the presence of the Goddess, with her wisdom, power and protection. The four cups on the left stand for law, the two on the right for love. **Divinatory meanings:** Happiness. Loving and being loved. Balance and peace. **Reversed:** The happy moment may be passing. Not recognizing happiness. Unbalanced or excessive behavior.

**SEVEN OF CUPS** 4 Youthful Folly. Six cups pointing upward symbolize the appearance of everything going well. The upside down cup in the center, however, tells that success and control are illusions. The card appears bright, but the bottom is dark. The background is a desert or perhaps a cave in the desert. **Divinatory meanings:** Beware of arrogance and complacency. Fantasies. **Reversed:** Hidden problems emerging. More realistic outlook.

**EIGHT OF CUPS** 41 Decrease. The cups are in confusion, reflecting chaos. Words on the lower right are from Chief Seattle's speech on the injustices done not only to humans but to animals and to Earth herself. Lines of light and flowing water give hope of a hidden joy that cannot be destroyed. **Divinatory meanings:** Failure. Arrogance and greed. Accept help from others. **Reversed:** Hidden joy. New happiness. Positive change.

**NINE OF CUPS** 42 Increase. Eight cups are in order. Nature has been restored and water is flowing through the rock. **Divinatory meanings:** Fortune. Wealth. Emotional breakthrough. Generosity. **Reversed:** Stinginess. Loss.

**TEN OF CUPS** 46 Pushing Upward. Stones push up from the surging sea. An ancient rock has a dark hole at its center, signifying mystery. The black dirt is fertile. **Divinatory meanings:** Successful development, with some effort required. **Reversed:** Success blocked. Negativity, apathy.

## THE SUIT OF SWORDS

**ACE OF SWORDS** The sword points down, the descent of sacred light into nature. The beginnings of green plants top the hill. The stirred up waves are the potential for life meeting active force. **Divinatory meanings:** Intelligence. Clear thinking. Powerful personality or emotions. **Reversed:** Anger. Aggression. Distorted thinking.

**TWO OF SWORDS** 11 Peace. Two swords are peacefully suspended in air. A temple pavilion is on the left. Two stone walls threaten the peace, along with the tinge of red on the moon. **Divinatory meanings:** Tranquility. Opportunity for prospering. **Reversed:** Disruption. Seek tranquility within.

**THREE OF SWORDS** 33 Retreat. From a wound, a single tear falls. The water emerges as a clear bubble, a symbol of the purification that comes through suffering. **Divinatory meanings:** Oppressive situations. Mourning. Sorrow. **Reversed:** Difficulty accepting loss. The natural cycle will bring renewal.

**FOUR OF SWORDS** 24 Return. The swords are suspended, creating a waiting feeling. A leaf falls slowly to the ground, and on it, a pearl or a bubble. A white feather on the ground in a woods signifies truce. **Divinatory meanings:** A moment of calm. **Reversed:** Movement away from silence and peace. New beginnings or old troubles.

**FIVE OF SWORDS** 47 Oppression. The broken swords represent technology. The ancient unicorn is dying. The bubble is tainted with blood. **Divinatory meanings:** An overwhelming situation. Need to hold onto principles until the time comes to make a change. **Reversed:** Situation growing better, with courage and persistence.

**SIX OF SWORDS** 61 Inner Truth. A hand reaches toward a leafless branch, part of a vineyard. Traces of green show that technology can bring new life to deserts. However, darkness beneath hints of something torn or broken. **Divinatory meanings:** Need for objectivity and honesty. **Reversed:** Idealism used for selfish ends.

**SEVEN OF SWORDS** 36 The Darkening of the Light. Faces melted together are the patriarchal power, the "useless old men" who arrange the world for their own benefit. The swords are scattered. **Divinatory meanings:** Depression. Possibly, the need to leave a situation for new possibilities. **Reversed:** Attempting to deal with feelings of uselessness.

**EIGHT OF SWORDS** 21 Biting Through. While the swords do not cut the trees, the trees appear ill. They symbolize nature in trouble, and a sick spirituality. A bright light shines on the trees and plants. **Divinatory meanings:** Interference. Gossip. Help or advice. **Reversed:** No interference. Avoiding responsibility.

**NINE OF SWORDS** 6 Conflict. A bird like the fantasy peacock of the two of cups is victim of the swords. The picture shows human cruelty. Part of an arm is from a picture of "The Three Graces," and shows the possibility of love and paradise. **Divinatory meanings:** Cruelty. Feeling like a victim. **Reversed:** Relief from cruel conditions. Confusion. Manipulation.

**TEN OF SWORDS** 29 The Abysmal. A destroyed city is a symbol of the modern world bringing its own ruin. But the clear sky shows a return to spiritual truths. The tips of the swords are broken. **Divinatory meanings:** Pain, confusion. Personal difficulties. Problems. **Reversed:** Troubles passing. Relief. Need to rest.

## THE SUIT OF STONES

**ACE OF STONES** The eagle landing on the rock is the two fundamental realms joined: Earth and sky, "ordinary" reality and spirit, feminine and masculine. The sky, the Earth, the rainbow are beauty and gifts. **Divinatory meanings:** Health. Prosperity. Beauty. Good weather. **Reversed:** Unappreciated gifts. Materialism. Conflicts over money or property.

**TWO OF STONES** 16 Enthusiasm. The fabric shows dark and light lines moving together. A hole signifies mystery, the unknown source of life. **Divinatory meanings:** Harmonic situations. **Reversed:** Disharmony. A time for solitude.

**THREE OF STONES** 13 Fellowship with Men. The background depicts a cross. The vertical line of spirit is strong, but the horizontal line of daily life is overgrown with fungus, indicating chaos. The cosmic balls show the possibility of great change. **Divinatory meanings:** Work. Satisfaction. **Reversed:** Work not going well. Unemployment. Laziness.

**FOUR OF STONES** 51 The Arousing. The background shows rocks in water. Tree roots are red, white, yellow and blue, signifying the four directions, which in turn signify Earth's power, physical and spiritual. The strips across the tree are mists rising from the water, signifying creative ideas. **Divinatory meanings:** Creativity and new ideas. Overwhelming energy. **Reversed:** Losing a sense of place. Fear.

**FIVE OF STONES** 23 Splitting Apart. Dead or dying

trees are before a pool of stagnant water. The stones float with no purpose or direction. The red spot can be a wound, or possibly life energy at the center of the dark time. A feather from a white bird reflects the beauty of winter. **Divinatory meanings:** Wintry time. Money troubles. Illness. Isolation. **Reversed:** Movement for the better. Wait, act cautiously.

**SIX OF STONES** 55 Abundance. The stones form two triangles. The center of the image is not a stone, but a hole in the cave. Golden light shines through the hole. **Divinatory meanings:** Great success and joy, possibly short-lived. Find inner truth in happiness. **Reversed:** Moment beginning to end. Save or invest money carefully during prosperity.

**SEVEN OF STONES** 12 Standstill. The stones have no pattern, as activity loses purpose without sacred connection. A sick tree bursts open, but the sky is clear, a sign of renewal. **Divinatory meanings:** Disharmony. Without careful redirection, failure is possible. **Reversed:** Recovery. Fresh start.

**EIGHT OF STONES** 62 Preponderance of the Small. The temple in the background, with its window, shows the physical world opening to something else. The stone elephant symbolizes the wisdom and knowledge of animals. **Divinatory meanings:** Be careful and moderate. Avoid excessive action. **Reversed:** Lack of moderation. Impatience. Ignorance.

**NINE OF STONES** 14 Possession in Great Measure. The pattern of the stones, balanced with the central stone close to the Earth, indicates progress and growth, but not constant. In the background is the sea and part of the roots of a great tree. **Divinatory meanings:** Fortune. Money, security, health, comfort. Avoid complacency, greed or conceit. **Reversed:** Misusing material gain. Greed.

**TEN OF STONES** 48 The Well. In a deep valley water rushes forth. Above the cleft of a rock is bright sky. **Divinatory meanings:** Good life. Health. A sense of solid reality. **Reversed:** Delay. Not appreciating material wealth and security.

# THE MINOR ARCANA: The Court Cards

**MOTHER OF WANDS** Kali's main color is black, for non-being. She wears a moon crown and has six limbs, the number of the Lovers. She is copulating with a dead Shiva, her consort. A snake winds around Shiva. Kali looms up huge in the sky, her feet on the Earth. **Divinatory meanings:** A wild, female energy. Dark power, sexual energy. **Reversed:** Kali-like energy suppressed. Destructiveness outweighs joy and love.

**FATHER OF WANDS** Brahma is the Creator in the Hindu Trimurti of Creator, Preserver, Destroyer. He has four arms, representing power beyond human limitations. His four faces blend. The cord on his chest and the white cloth signify the priestly caste. A scroll in one hand is religious laws, a cup holds milk, and a spoon is to stir the milk over the sacred fire. **Divinatory meanings:** A calm person, possibly stuffy. A rooted quality that gives strength. **Reversed:** Snobbishness, especially intellectual. Devotion. Doubts, weakness, confusion.

**DAUGHTER OF WANDS** Radha and Krishna (son of wands) are gods, but they are also human. They are young and in love. Their flutes are the power of wands translated into music. Radha's flute blends the colors of the rainbow. The red dot on her forehead is a symbol of holiness and life. Three stones over her forehead signify sensuality, motherhood and wisdom. **Divinatory meanings:** Abundance. Joy. Good sense. Culture. **Reversed:** Unfulfilled potential.

**SON OF WANDS** The blue halo behind Krishna symbolizes the eye of a peacock feather. Krishna's flute music brings the divine mind into physical reality. **Divinatory meanings:** Love of life. Interest in the arts. Trickster. Attractiveness. **Reversed:** Difficulty. Conflict. Problems may bring out depths in a person.

**MOTHER OF CUPS** The legs of the ancient stone image shown on the mother of cups go into the ground. The "Venus" is of the Earth. The moon and the ocean connect her with the Goddess. The landscape is green and fertile. **Divinatory meanings:** Earthy, plain, honest person. Matriarch. Ancient forces. **Reversed:** Someone out of touch with physical realities.

**FATHER OF CUPS** Odin hangs from the World Tree in order to bring up the runes from the dark well of Mimir. He has offered one of his eyes to Mimir. **Divinatory meanings:** A powerful, domineering person. Intelligence. Creativity. Generous and loving. **Reversed:** Father's power disrupted.

**DAUGHTER OF CUPS** Brigid was a goddess of the Celts. When she was made a saint by Christian Ireland, she became patron of livestock and produce, as well as of poetry, prophecy and divination. **Divinatory meanings:** Calmness and radiance. Peacefulness and strength of character. **Reversed:** Loss of self-assurance. Importance of personal history ignored.

**SON OF CUPS** Parsival stares at the Grail in astonishment, even shock. He discovers spiritual truth, along with his responsibility to help restore the Earth. He is like Christ waking up to the divine reality that will lead to his own crucifixion. **Divinatory meanings:** Sweet-tempered, but naive person. A good heart. A test. **Reversed:** Avoiding responsibility. Callousness.

**MOTHER OF SWORDS** Nut is the night sky, arched over the Earth. She also appears to be standing upright on her toes, as she would appear painted on the inner lid of a sarcophagus. The stars resemble a human with arms and legs out in celebration. **Divinatory meanings:** A mysterious person. Devotion. Autonomy. **Reversed:** Need for privacy exaggerated. Conflict between love of solitude and love for others.

**FATHER OF SWORDS** The deadly snake, the uraeus or asp, curls around the sun. Though the snake kills, its green color indicates the mystery of rebirth. The sun is order and law, and the principle of energy. Ra carries a scepter, symbol of his power. **Divinatory meanings:** Dominant, autocratic person. Delegating authority to others. Strong, creative intellect. Fairness. **Reversed:** Tyrant. A person jealous of personal power.

**DAUGHTER OF SWORDS** Isis's hair falls like water. She is mother of pharaohs; an abstract throne crowns her. Above her third eye, the cobra connects the king to spiritual powers. Hathor the cow goddess is on the right. She is the goddess of love, dance and ecstasy. **Divinatory meanings:** A powerful figure, confident and dynamic. **Reversed:** Loss of confidence. Depression.

**SON OF SWORDS** Osiris is a peaceful ruler; his crook and flail indicate his power derives from his role as teacher of agriculture. He is in white, as the first mummy and the lord of the afterworld. **Divinatory meanings:** Someone gentle yet persuasive. An initiate into esoteric mysteries. Kindness. **Reversed:** Weakness, possibly corruption.

**MOTHER OF STONES** The serene face of Spider Woman, the mother, radiates the labyrinth of her thoughts. The woman stands unmoving against a background in which the Earth and the sky seem to join. The labyrinth forms a spiral. **Divinatory meanings:** Serene, probably older woman. Self-confidence. **Reversed:** Difficulty in staying still and appreciating life. Loss of personal center.

**FATHER OF STONES** The footprints of animals and the dark prints of a Spirit being show on the ground. The Old Man is a helper Spirit for the Earth. **Divinatory meanings:** Fundamental male principle. Someone who cares deeply for family and for nature. Hard worker. **Reversed:** Cold and uncaring. Lack of success. Pain at the suffering of the world.

**DAUGHTER OF STONES** The daughter is against a background of rock. A golden light around her head is sacred energy. The pipe symbolizes the cosmos. According to the Native American visionary Black Elk, the White Buffalo Woman was a mystical woman who taught the people rituals and brought them the pipe. **Divinatory meanings:** Willingness to take responsibility for something greater than oneself. Love, courage and dedication. Inner beauty. **Reversed:** Difficulty getting across ideas or emotions. Feeling out of place.

**SON OF STONES** Chief Seattle was one of the last leaders of a nation of Native Americans on the northwest coast of North America. His hair blends into the rock. The eagle feather, a symbol of the Plains peoples, indicates that he spoke for all Natives. The lightning bolt from the whale above shows the bond between human and animal. **Divinatory meanings:** Taking action to make positive change—with the benefit of the next seven generations in mind. **Reversed:** Despair. Selfishness leads to feeling lost.

## MEDITATION

Meditation with the tarot allows us to create a personal bond between ourselves and the cards. It takes us directly to the heart of the image, allowing us to make it a part of our own lives, our own knowledge.

To begin your meditation, choose a time and place where you can sit without disturbance. Sit comfortably, with your back straight. Be peaceful and calm; close your eyes and let your breathing become deep and natural. Do not force it; every point of meditation is a natural, relaxed process. Feel yourself begin to relax.

Take the card into your hand and look at it. Do not analyze it or memorize any of its official meanings. Allow yourself to experience its qualities.

Now put the card down and close your eyes. Let yourself relax; do not try to remember what you were thinking. Allow the image of the card to enter your mind. As you breathe in, let the qualities of the card fill you. As you breathe out, experience those qualities moving through your whole body. When you feel you have spent enough time, take a final deep breath and when you release it, open your eyes.

Sit for a while longer before you go back to your daily activities. Pick up the card again and refresh your mind with its image.

During your first tries at meditation, you may get distracted, or your mind will wander, and nothing at all seems to happen between you and the card. Unless you actively dislike it, keep trying. Slowly you will discover that your relaxation is deeper, your contact with the cards more intense, and your experiences more personal. The relaxation by itself calms the nerves, renews the body and opens up the breath. It also makes room for the spiritual messages contained within the cards.

# THE HAGALL SPREAD

The Hagall Spread forms the shape of the rune Hagall, which means "hailstone," and forms the pattern of the universe.

Separate the cards into Major Arcana, suit cards (numbered Minor Arcana) and court cards. Shuffle the suit cards, thinking of the question you have. Turn over four suit cards in a diamond pattern (cards 1-4 in diagram).

**1:** The general situation.

**2:** Something you've done, or an experience you've had, that has helped create the current situation.

**3:** Your beliefs—impressions and expectations, conscious or subconscious, of the situation.

**4:** The likely result of the situation as things stand now.

Next shuffle the Major Arcana and lay down three in a triangle above the Minor cards (cards 5-7 in the diagram). The Major Arcana indicate our spiritual tasks.

**5:** Spiritual history, how you've behaved, what you've learned.

**6:** Spiritual task at this time, the challenges and opportunities in the current situation.

**7:** Metamorphosis, how the situation will change and the spiritual tasks that will come to you as a result.

Now shuffle the court cards and lay them out in a row below the others (cards 8-10 in the diagram). The court cards in the Hagall spread are always read upright. If any come out reversed (upside down), turn them around before reading them.

**8:** The Helper. Visualize the actual person. This person gives you total support.

**9:** Yourself. You are expressing the qualities of the person shown on the card.

**10:** The Teacher. This figure can indicate the demands of the situation, and also the knowledge that you can gain from the situation.

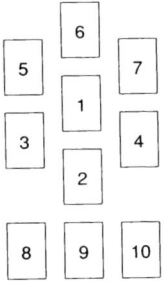

**The Hagall Spread**

For our complete line of tarot decks,
books, meditation cards, oracle sets,
and other inspirational products
please visit our website:

**www.usgamesinc.com**

**Follow us on:**

U.S. GAMES SYSTEMS, INC.
179 Ludlow Street
Stamford, CT 06902 USA
Phone: 203-353-8400
Order Desk: 800-544-2637
Fax: 203-353-8431